Skateboarding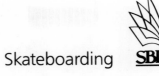

SKATEBOARDING

Florian Böhm & Marcus Rieger

 SBL Springfield Books Limited

© Falken Verlag GmbH 1990

First published 1990 by
Falken Verlag GmbH
6275 Niedernhausen, Germany

This edition first published 1991
by Springfield Books Limited,
Norman Road, Denby Dale
Huddersfield HD8 8TH
West Yorkshire, England.

British Library Cataloguing
in Publication Data
Böhm, Florian
Skateboard.
1. Skateboarding
I. Title   II. Rieger, Markus
796.21

ISBN 0-947655-98-0

Cover design: Douglas Martin
Translation: Andrew Shackleton
Typesetting:
Armitage Typo/Graphics Ltd
Huddersfield
Printed and bound in Hong Kong
by Colorcraft

UK pro, Neil Danns, does an *ollie fakie*

Acknowledgements

The publishers are grateful to the following people for supplying additional material for use in this book:

Paul Duffy, for supplying pictures for the cover and pages 4-5 and 6.

Steve Kane, for advising on the technical aspects of Skateboarding.

Contents

Anders Pulpaneck, competing in the World
Cup at Münster, Germany

The raddest thing on wheels

Vancouver 1986: an artist's impression

Jan Waage in an *ollie grab to fakie*

Skateboarding is as mad as the people that practise it. A skateboard may be no more than a board with two trucks and four wheels, but it has spawned a whole youth culture that has spread over two continents.

Skateboarding means speed, fun and excitement. A skateboard is not so much a means of getting from A to B, or a mere item of sports equipment – it is a whole philosophy of life. Skateboarding is the ultimate answer to the drab, grey surroundings of modern life. It gives a feeling of freedom and independence.

As you streak down the sidewalk on your skateboard, you feel superior to everyone else. As you speed past other people, you feel the adrenalin flowing, and you and your board become totally at one. Nobody who has not been on a skateboard can appreciate this feeling.

The two most important words in the skateboarder's dictionary are 'speed' and 'radness'. A skateboarder can let out all his aggressions, while at the same time

Sidewalk surfing in California

A "self-portrait" by Florian Böhm at the Berlin Bowl

...aking sure that no one else ...injured or put at risk. ...Radness' means a ...kateboarder's total ...edication to his sport. ...e must always be ready to ...ush himself to the furthest ...mits.

'Skate and destroy' was ...e slogan put out in the ...arly eighties by the San ...rancisco skateboard journal ...hrasher Magazine. ...his wasn't a call to blind ...estructiveness but a way of ...adicalising the sport. 'Push ...e limits' was another ...opular slogan, reflecting ...e same spirit of speed and ...dventure. When you get ...nto your skateboard, you ...nter a whole new world of ...leas and fantasies. When ...ou ride it to the limits, a vast range of new possibilities opens up before you.

Skateboarding philosophy is also reflected in other ways. The clothes that skateboarders wear mark them out as belonging to a special group, and the same applies to the way that they talk. Outsiders have difficulty understanding all the jargon — even the slogans on their T-shirts are a closed book. But for skateboarders they all have a special significance — they sum up a whole lifestyle.

Skateboarders are not anarchists; they are just a group apart from the 'normal' world. Some people look on skate-boarding as an alternative existence, while others see it only as a passing fashion that has lasted longer than some. We could go into the arguments on this, but that is not what this book is for. Our object here is to give you the basics of this new and fast-developing sport.

The history of skateboarding

The development of the skateboard: from the simple sidewalk surfer (top left) with no kicktail and the wheels sticking out, via the slalom board (bottom left) made partly out of aluminium, to the modern pro board (bottom left) with its kicktail, concave and various other essentials

Skateboarding may be a young sport, but its origins are shrouded in mystery. Stories abound on the skateboarding scene, but the fact is that no one knows for sure who invented it and where. It probably began some time in the late fifties on the surfing beaches of California, when someone hit on the idea of attaching a pair of rollerskates to a surfboard.

Skateboarding at first would have been no more than a kind of 'sidewalk surfing' — the nearest thing to real surfing when the waves weren't high enough. That would also explain why the first skateboarders went barefoot.

The origins of skateboarding are reflected in the design of the first skateboards, which were closely modelled on surfboards. They were fairly narrow — only about four inches (ten centimetres) wide — and a good deal shorter than the skateboards of today. The riders stood on the board in bare feet, in a more sideways stance than today. They would have done little more than ride up and down the sidewalk, steering the board by simply leaning to the left or right.

The first major development came with the invention of the **kicktail**: an extra area of board behind the rear truck (axle). If you push down on the kicktail, the front of the board rises slightly off the ground. This allows the board to be steered more easily while in motion.

The first boom: pools and skateparks

The first manufactured skateboards came onto the market in 1965. These usually consisted of inch-thick wooden boards with narrow cast-iron trucks and hard-rubber wheels. The faces along the sidewalk were varied in different ways, and soon the first competition events appeared: freestyle, slalom, downhill, high jump and long jump. Skateboarding was starting to develop as a sport in its own right.

In the mid-seventies skaters began to try new routes along drainage channels and up the slopes around buildings. This opened a whole new world of tricks. They had discovered bank skating, out of which vertical skating was later to develop. Skaters were also learning to move their bodies more skilfully, and soon they were able to defy gravity.

Vertical skating began in the backyard pools of California. These were

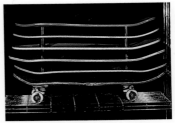

Modern profile decks

empty swimming pools, which, unlike those in Europe, had rounded sides. All you needed was a bit of extra speed, and you could ride your board up the pool side as far as the edge.

There were a number of problems here. Firstly the pool owners often didn't like their pools being used in this way. And secondly the pool sides weren't quite rounded enough. These so-called transitions went vertical much too suddenly, almost catapulting the rider into the air. It was very difficult to get back down safely, and by then you were riding too slowly to make it up the opposite side of the pool.

But skateboarding developed quickly in the United States, and it wasn't long before the first skateparks appeared. These were specially laid out with the skateboarder in mind. Pools were built with extra-rounded sides, and there were other layouts for bank and freestyle skating.

◀ First-generation sidewalk surfers

Boomer Ramp in the Raging Waters Pleasure Park. Shaped like a boomerang, it is one of California's largest halfpipes

Up until the early eighties these were the main meeting places for skateboarders. Competitions and tournaments were organised around them. Pool and vertical skate-boarding became the most popular specialist forms.

Vert skating, as it came to be known, was the most spectacular form. It was extremely difficult and demanding, and this encouraged even more innovations in board manufacture. The boards were built wider to give the rider more stability. New polyurethane wheels proved

faster than the old rubber ones, and they also had more grip.

By now, barefoot skating was confined to a few die-hard sidewalk surfers. Most skaters had realised that gymshoes gave more stability, not to mention protection when you fell off the board.

Hard times: halfpipe and street

By 1980, skateboarding had swept across Europe, where the most popular disciplines were freestyle, slalom and

high jump. But on both sides of the Atlantic it was still thought of as a passing craze, and was not taken seriously as a competitive sport.

The early eighties saw a sudden slump in popularity. It almost happened within a single season: skateparks closed their gates, board manufacturers stopped production, and skateboard magazines turned to BMX and rollerskating. But a small band of enthusiasts kept the flag flying in both continents. They continued to develop their techniques they produced their own magazine, made some of their own boards and built their own layouts.

This was the time when the first halfpipes (as we now call them) appeared on the scene. These were simpler and cheaper to build than pools, and could be designed by skaters themselves. They also gave scope for a whole series of new tricks. Halfpipes are usually built of wood, and are effectively U-shaped with a ten-foot radius transition on either side. The flat area in between is wide enough to give you time to concentrate and get up speed before mounting the other side.

The sport was becoming unpopular with the general public, and this pushed the skateboarding scene

Gerd Rieger crusing over a bank layout in Hagen, Germany

Upland Skatepark in California, closed in 1989 because of insurance problems, had one of the world's steepest pools

Kele Rosecrans the American Shredder does a *layback*

underground'. You might
have thought this would
have stifled it, but if anything
the opposite happened.
Skateboard culture became
smaller but more
committed, and entered one
of its most creative phases.
   Skateboard enthusiasts
became so involved that
their whole life revolved
around the sport. It was not
so much a sport as a lifestyle
in its own right — a whole
new philosophy of life.
Without such commitment
the sport could never have
survived. The few remaining
skaters injected a new idealism
into the organisation of their
events, and showed the same
drive in the publication of
their own magazines and
the smaller 'skate zines'.

Above: Cedar Crest Ramp was one of America's first large halfpipes

Below: Florian Böhm performing a *backside air* at Kona, one of Florida's old skateparks

Christian Hosoi doing a *street ollie*

Steve Claar doing a *ramp ollie*

Skateboarding soon developed into a new method of transport. Skaters would tackle any route, mount any obstacle that came their way. They would use their board anywhere and everywhere they could. Thus in the early eighties the art of street skating came about.

The street skater was completely independent of halfpipes and other artificial layouts; he was his own man. Tricks that only vert skaters had used were adapted to the street. Street ollies, slide 'n' rolls and kerb grinds are the classic street moves, and all of them came from vert skating.

Street skating was soon turned into a competition discipline, which from then on became known as street style. It soon proved impossible to create a competition layout that was really like a street. So today's street-style events are a cross between ramp skating and street skating, and are more often called obstacle contests.

But street is still one of the most popular forms of skateboarding. Every skateboarder is really a street skater at heart, because this is where his roots lie. It's just that some skaters have forgotten one or two things along the way.

Skateboarding comes of age

In 1985 skateboarding started to become popular with the public again. The sport was emerging from the shadows, and there were the beginnings of a second skateboard boom.

Street style attracted lots of new young skaters, and the lifestyle philosophy of hardcore skaters soon became particularly attractive to kids.

Lance Mountain in a *tailslide*

Dirk Wehnes performs a *handrail slide*

Since then sporting performance has improved by leaps and bounds. The Americans have set new standards, especially in vert skating and street style. Tricks are becoming more radical than ever, and techniques are continually being refined. Years of training are needed to master them, and the whole scene is becoming much more professional.

A wallride bank in the foreground, a funbox in the middle and a quarterpipe bank at the ba

Recent developments

Miniramp skating is the latest addition to the sport. A miniramp is like a small halfpipe except that the walls aren't vertical. It is particularly suited to beginners who aren't yet ready to tackle verticals.

The miniramp has brought with it a whole new set of tricks.

Meanwhile, some disciplines have become less popular than before. Among them are slalom and high jump.

In the late eighties skateboarding was at last accepted as a real sport on the world stage, and now it can no longer be dismissed as a passing fad. There is a lucrative professional circuit both in the United States and in Europe, and spectators can be numbered in their tens of thousands.

Claus Grabke performs a *slide 'n' roll* in the halfpipe during the 1987 World Cup in Münster, Germany

reat skaters

 history of skateboarding complete without at least me mention of its heroes. ey have not only shaped e sport, but without them would not be around day. Some of these people ve become cult figures in eir own right.

The legendary **Tony Alva** as the first pool shredder. e was the world long-jump cord-holder for many ars after clearing seven drums in one go. **Stacy eralta,** like Tony Alva, now s his own make of ateboard, but in the early ys he too was one of the ost successful pool skaters.

Another of the all-time eats was the master of saster himself, **Duane ters** from the United ates. He was the first of e truly radical skaters. e pushed the limits with thought for his board or r himself. Duane Peters as the first skater to anage a complete loop in fullpipe — a tube with diameter of 18 feet .5 metres) — riding rough the first totally pside-down position. is commitment is shown the fact that he only anaged it on the third ttempt, having fallen out f the highest position on e previous two attempts.

Also worth mentioning e the three vert skaters

Rodney Mullen

Steve Caballero, Mike McGill and **Tony Hawk.** They have been competing for more than ten years, but they are still among the world's greatest riders. Steve, for example, is the great master of style and perfection. He's a true artist, and his rides are a feast for the eyes.

Steve Caballero

Mike McGill is best known for a legendary trick that he invented known as the 540-degree McTwist. This is an air (aerial trick) involving a somersault with a half twist. He first achieved it at the 1985 Swedish Summer Camp, opening up a whole new world of tricks. It is still one of the most difficult moves in the sport.

Tony Hawk

Tony Hawk has for years been the most successful skater in the world. He has won more championships, and invented more tricks than anyone else. He also has the largest feet. This may be the key to his success, but no one knows for sure, even Tony himself. Tony is the one who's setting the standards in the skateboarding world.

Equipment

THE SKATEBOARD

A skateboard consists of three main parts: the deck, the two trucks and the four wheels.

The deck is covered with a grip tape made of a material like sandpaper. It can be further protected with a nosebone at the front and a tailbone at the back. These are plastic mountings that stop the wood from splitting. But they aren't often used these days because in vert skating they can get in the way.

Each truck (axle) consists of a hanger (the cross-piece between the two wheels), two rubbers (to help with steering), a kingpin (to give vertical stability) and a baseplate (mounted under the deck for fixing the hanger). Each wheel also has two bearings with a spacer between them.

Choice of board

There are so many differen makes of skateboard that the range can be confusin even for an expert. And if you're new to the sport, yo will certainly need some guidance when buying a board. So here are some ti about the kinds of things 1 look out for.

There are two distinct categories of board: the fu professional board and the cheap board that you can buy in a supermarket. The difference in price is quite amazing, but it reflects a similar difference in qualit A professional set-up cost around £100, whereas a cheap one may cost no more than £10. Why shou this be?

There are two reasons why the supermarket boards are so cheap. Firstl most of them are made in the Far East, and secondly the construction is very primitive. To the newcome they don't look very differe from a professional board But they are heavier, made of cheaper wood, and the deck is flat rather than concave. The wheels are o softer material than the

The components of a skateboard

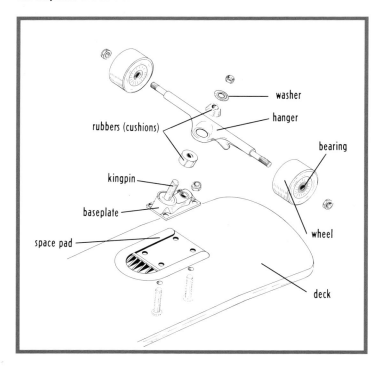

rubbers (cushions)

washer

hanger

kingpin

bearing

baseplate

wheel

space pad

deck

andard polyurethane, so ey turn much more slowly. e truck tends to be more id, and on some models e kingpin sticks out from e hanger.

It's not always a mistake buy a cheap board at st. You can't tell whether u're serious about ateboarding until you've ed it out for a bit. Some ung people get bored ter a few weeks, and £100 a lot to shell out for a ssing phase. But if you cide you're really serious, en a professional board is e only sensible solution the long run.

Professional boards are ually only available in rts, but most specialist alers will be happy to ild one for you. Nearly per cent of the uipment and parts come m the United States.

The **deck** comes in at ast 500 different ofessional models. rofessional' means they e sold in the name of a ofessional skater, who uches for the quality and ape of the deck and gets mmission on every one ld.

A good deck is usually ade up of six or seven thin yers of hardrock maple. ese layers are glued gether with the grain nning alternately ossways and lengthways

to ensure that the deck is stable, and are then welded together under pressure.

Most decks have a slightly dished shape, known as the concave, which gives more stability by making your feet less likely to slip off. This, together with the grip tape, means that your feet effectively stick to the board, even in the halfpipe.

The deck is usually measured in inches, and it must be the correct length for the height of the rider. The normal pro deck is 30.5 inches (about 77 centimetres) long, and is ideal for riders over five foot six (1.7 metres). Most pro models have a so-called mini version measuring 28.5 inches (71.5 centimetres), which is ideal for younger skaters.

People often ask if there are quality differences between the various American makes of pro deck. There are certainly differences, but you can't tell them just from the price. It's virtually impossible to say in general terms which makes are good and which are bad. The best way of finding out is to ask around on the scene about which makes are strongest and which have the best concave.

Too many inexperienced skaters are taken in by the pro image of a deck, or simply decide from the look of the thing. Neither of

these methods is a reliable way of finding a good board.

The trucks

In general, all American-style pro skateboard trucks are strong enough to stand the pressure. But they do vary in their steering capabilities. Some are better suited to skaters who like a board with firm steering for extra stability. Other skaters

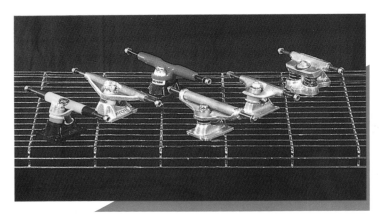

Different kinds of truck

prefer a truck that responds more quickly, but this also requires more skill.

Most pro trucks are made of cast aluminium alloy with steel axles, and are guaranteed to last, unlike the cheaper ones. Some companies have experimented with magnesium alloy to make the truck lighter, but this is more expensive and less reliable than the standard product.

Make sure that you buy trucks of the correct length for your board. When the wheels are mounted, they should be exactly flush with the side of the board.

The wheels

These vary in size as well as hardness. They usually measure between 57 and 67 millimetres in diameter, and the choice will depend on your height and your individual preference. But

Make sure the truck matches the deck. The truck below has been worn and grooved by grinds along kerbs and metal copings, but this won't adversely affect performance as long as there are no actual cracks

the hardness grade is more important to get exactly right. Some manufacturers provide durometer readings, which give the hardness on a graduated scale from one to 100. The wheels available nowadays measure between 85 and 98 on this scale.

What are the best makes of skateboard wheel? The answer will depend on the particular discipline you choose and the kind of surface you're likely to ride on. As a rule of thumb, the

harder the wheel, the faster it goes but the less grip it has

Freestyle wheels are normally the smallest, measuring 57 millimetres and with a hardness grade of 97. They have to be smaller because there isn't usually a space pad mounted between the deck and the truck. If they were larger they would tend to touch the deck when you turn or stop suddenly.

Street wheels should have a hardness grade of between 95 and 97. A 95 provides the ideal grip on tarmac, but it rather slower than the 97.

For the halfpipe the standard 97 is best. It's ideally suited to wooden ramps and concrete pools, as it provides plenty of speed without too much loss of grip. The exception to this is a metal ramp or a pool with very smooth concrete, where a 95 is much better. But if a halfpipe is covered with a new layer of beech (or any other wood with a good

A badly worn wheel

The diameter and hardness are usually given on the side of the wheel

grip), then you can even use a 98, which is much harder and faster.

Maintenance

Whatever you may think, the bearings are pre-greased, and you don't need to oil them. All you will do is to make them unnecessarily dirty, and it won't make the wheels any quicker either. All you need to do is to wipe them clean with a cloth from time to time.

A skateboard needs surprisingly little maintenance. Every now and then you will need to tighten the screws on the truck mountings. This is because the parts wear at different rates.

Street wheels are more prone to wear, as has already been mentioned. They quickly lose speed during the first couple of weeks of use, but then they stay much the same for a long time. You shouldn't keep replacing them, because the loss of speed has no effect on the way they run.

The trucks again need very little maintenance, though the rubbers will need replacing if they start to split. Trucks only break rarely, and they could last the whole of your skating career.

The weakest part of the skateboard is the deck. It lasts much longer than it used to, thanks to new laminating techniques in manufacture. But this doesn't change the fact that wood is a rather soft material. You can't avoid at least some damage. The commonest problem is splitting at the nose and tail, together with scratches and other minor abrasions.

Occasionally a deck actually breaks in two, but this is nearly always due to ill treatment. The commonest place for such a break is immediately in front of the rear truck. This is a sure sign that the rider has landed wrongly after falling from a height. For example, if you jump down from the top of a jump ramp, you should always bend your knees to cushion your landing. If you keep your legs straight, then the board has to withstand a force several times the weight of your body. So no wonder the deck breaks at the point that is under most stress.

The nose and tail are the weakest parts; the wood here is liable to split

Nearly every item to do with a skateboard can be bought individually at a specialist shop. Such things include rubbers in various colours and grades of hardness, different kinds of grip tape and all the components of a truck. Again, the choice can be bewildering.

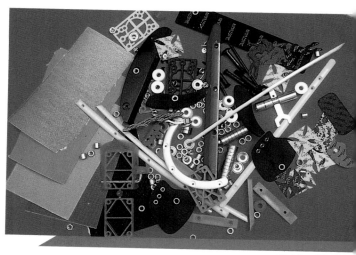

Skateboard hardware

CLOTHING AND ACCESSORIES

Apart from the all-important components, there is a wide range of so-called skateboard accessories. These include all the lifestyle gear such as bags, T-shirts, rucksacks, shoes and lots more. Even keyrings, watches and sunglasses are supplied in special skateboarding designs.

The whole skateboard market has become highly commercialised. So if you're new to the scene, don't let anybody talk you into buying anything you don't want or you don't need. All you actually need is a good board, a sensible pair

of shoes and a suitable range of protective gear.

Shoes

Footwear is one area where the industry has got it right, as there is a wide range of good shoes available. The first thing is a good rubber sole; it must have a good grip, and must be so shaped that the foot is well positioned on the board. Hightops are the best kind of shoe, covering the ankles and with plenty of support around the heel and the ankles.

Lifestyle gear

As for the rest of the gear, you won't know what you fancy until you've been around on the scene for a bit. Have a good look round before you decide to buy a

Skateboard accessories

24

veatshirt advertising this or at company, or that you'd ther have a video of the ntest in South Uzbekistan, that you can't sleep until u've found a wall poster pro Joe Bloggs in action. all up to you.

ective gear at a glance

ROTECTIVE GEAR

e following items of otective gear are required r skateboarding: helmet, bow pads, kneepads and oves or wristguards. In the d days people sometimes ore hip pads as well.

Pads are an expensive m when you first learn ateboarding, but saving oney on them is a false conomy in the long run. ithout them you're simply t safe, and safety is a imary consideration in ateboarding just as in her sports.

Always buy top-quality oducts from specialist ealers, and avoid anything o cheap. You may have to y out more, but it's worth

the expense just to stay in one piece.

You won't need all the gear for every skateboarding event. A pair of kneepads is good enough for freestyle, and if you start on the street all you'll need is a pair of kneepads and a stout pair of gloves. But for a miniramp or halfpipe nothing less than the full complement will do.

Knee and elbow pads

Kneepads are the most important item of protective gear. They must always be worn, whatever the discipline. Elbow pads are less vital, but work on much the same principle.

A good kneepad is made up of several elements. The inside section around the

knee itself consists of several layers of a neoprene-like foam, which is usually covered by a layer of nylon material. This acts as a shock-absorber, providing almost total protection from any impact. The outside consists of a plastic cap that has been riveted on. This allows the kneepad to slide harmlessly down a halfpipe after a bail (fall).

The components of a kneepad

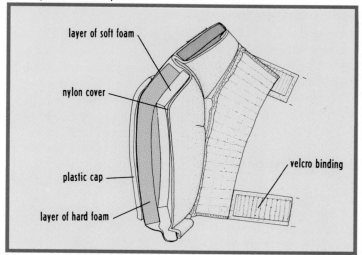

layer of soft foam

nylon cover

plastic cap

layer of hard foam

velcro binding

A new gadget has recently been invented to stop the kneepads slipping. It is known as a knee gasket, and consists of a thin layer of neoprene that is worn underneath the kneepad. This ensures that the pad always stays in place over the knee.

Kneepads are vital for a technique known as knee sliding, which is most often needed for a bail in the halfpipe. If you find you can't stay upright for a trick, then you fall onto the plastic caps on your kneepads and slide down the transition to the flat part of the halfpipe. The kneepads will protect your knees from injury.

Helmet

The helmet is particularly vital in the halfpipe. The outside consists of a hard plastic shell, while the inside is made of a firm foam material. Make sure your helmet is the correct size for your head. If it's too large, it will be no use in a fall as it will simply come off.

Wristguards or gloves?

All that remains is to decide whether to wear wristguards or gloves. There are good arguments on both sides. Wristguards are essential

A wristguard

for vert skating, as the wrist is the most vulnerable part in any fall in the halfpipe. A wristguard provides support by means of two hard plastic splints, one above and one below. The two are firmly linked together with ripstop nylon or leather straps.

Wristguards limit movement to some extent, so gloves are needed for tricks that need more freedom of movement such as inverts (see page 78). But in general wristguards give better protection, so should always be preferred.

Gloves protect the palms of the hands instead of the wrists. They should always be worn for street skating so as to avoid nasty grazes when you fall on the tarmac.

Other safety measures

You can't protect yourself from injury in all cases. There will always be occasional sprains, fractures and torn ligaments. Beginners are often the most at risk, as they often overestimate their abilities. But there are ways of making injuries less serious, and your skating will be less dangerous if you observe the following four safety points:

➼ Always warm up thoroughly before every session, using stretching exercises or the like.
➼ Always wear plenty of protective gear, even if everyone else tells you it isn't 'cool'
➼ Learn to fall properly as soon as you can.
➼ Never try the halfpipe until you've learned to control the board in all situations on the ground.

If you observe these four points, you will reduce the risk of injury to a minimum.

How to bail: step forward off the board front foot first, brake your fall on the transition, and slide down gently on your kneepads; land safely on your kneepads and the top of your shoes

Riding practice

Pushing off

There are usually two main questions in people's minds when they start skating for the first time: what are the pitfalls to look out for, and what are the basic skills that you need? But before we go on to answer these questions, there are one or two other points to note.

Firstly, the front of the board is known as the nose, and the back is known as the kicktail, or simply the tail. And just as there are left-handed and right-handed writers, and footballers who shoot from the right or the left, so there are some skaters who stand with their left foot on the tail and others with the right foot. Skaters make an important distinction here. The ones who ride with the left foot in front are described as **regular-footed,** while those that lead with the right foot are known as **goofy-footed.**

As you follow the descriptions and picture sequences for each trick, check whether the particular skater is regular o goofy-footed, and ask yourself whether you are the same or the opposite way round. But remember that the movements are the same, whichever way round

Stepping onto the board

Here's what to do when you first step onto the board; the first time you do this, you should hold on to a wall, a fence or another kater, and make sure the board is both level and stationary:

→ First put your front foot on the board just behind the front truck and pointing at an angle. At this point you should be leaning mainly on your back foot, which is still firmly on the ground.

→ Now move your weight onto your front foot and place your back foot on the tail in the concave about a centimetre in front of the back edge; keep your toes on the board, but don't worry if the heel sticks out.

Never put your back foot on before the front foot, or the board will shoot off like a rocket and you'll end up in a heap on the ground.

Pushing off

To set the board in motion, take your back foot off the tail and push off from the ground using the ball of your back foot. While in motion always keep your weight over the front foot. If you want to get up speed, keep your weight over the front foot and keep pushing off the ground in a regular rhythm.

Turning

You can do this by leaning your body into the turn.

Stopping the board

Turn right or left . . .

. . . by leaning inwards or outwards

Start in the basic riding position (with your knees and hips slightly bent), and lean your body forwards or backwards, pressing with your toes or your heels on the edge of the board. The board will turn right or left.

Braking

There are two ways of braking safely. The first is to take your back foot off the tail and slide it along the ground until you come to a standstill. The other is to step forwards off the board.

The second method is more difficult than the first. You take your back foot off the tail and run forwards, gradually slowing down. This stops the board more quickly than the first method, but it will need plenty of practice at slow speeds.

Keep practising

When you first start skating, you should practise all these techniques thoroughly until you have the board completely under your control.

Here is a summary of the main points:

→ Step safely onto the board, and always with your front foot first.

→ Get your balance before you start moving.

Braking by running forwards off the board. Take your back foot off the board first so that you can step over the nose and slow down the board by running out in front of it

⌐ Start moving by pushing off with your back foot.

⌐ Turn the board by leaning your body and pushing on the side edge.

⌐ Brake by sliding your back foot along the ground or stepping forwards off the board.

Once you've mastered these basic skills, you can start having some fun cruising up and down the street. Then after a bit more practice you can try out a few slopes and get a feel for riding at speed. But by this stage you should be able to brake without even having to think about it.

The kickturn

The next technique you'll need to learn is a kickturn on the ground. This is basically a way of moving forward simply by shifting your body.

The kicktail plays an important role in this.

⌐ Press down slightly on the tail with your back foot, and the front wheels will lift slightly off the ground.

⌐ At the same time turn the board by twisting your body 45 degrees to the right.

⌐ Now lean forward again onto your front foot, and the front wheels will return to the ground.

A kickturn requires good foot coordination: press on the tail with your back foot to raise the nose, turn the board with your front foot in the direction you want, and the board will be propelled forward

Mike Manzourie in the miniramp doing an *ollie tailgrab*

the most popular events, often with 100 or more skaters at the start. Freestyle skaters are the smallest group, but they make up for this in solidarity. In freestyle everyone knows each other, and everybody has a feeling of belonging.

Halfpipe is the king of all the disciplines. It's fantastic to watch and makes heavy demands on the skaters. As for miniramp, we can't yet be sure how it will develop, but it shows every sign of having a following as large as street style.

Skateboard events have an atmosphere of their own, and it's difficult to compare them with other sports. Skateboarding is more a scene than a club sport. Very few skaters belong to clubs, so only a few events are actually organised by clubs. Skaters always turn up in their own gear, and club

Young Rasmus Skoussen in the street event at the 1989 European Championships in Madrid

- ⊶ Do the whole thing again, but this time turn to the left.
- ⊶ Keep repeating the whole process, turning alternately right and left, and the board will move forward and gather speed.

THE COMPETITION DISCIPLINES

The European competition scene has undergone a lot of changes in the last ten years.

It has mainly followed the American model, but at the same time it has developed a style all of its own.

The main disciplines are the same as those in America: freestyle, street and halfpipe. But European amateurs and professionals usually set off in groups, and freestyle is considered more important here than in America. Miniramp became an official discipline in America in 1988, two years earlier than in Europe.

Street competitions are

niforms and start numbers
e out.

Competitions are
rganised by a whole variety
f bodies. These may include
cal authorities, skatepark
anagers or even
presentatives of the
ateboard industry.

There are few specialist
ateboarding coaches. In
ct skaters don't usually talk
bout training so much as
bout communal sessions,
hich are for fun as much as
r learning. Sometimes a
ater learns his own
pertoire of tricks, and
ometimes groups of skaters
ow off their latest tricks to
ach other.

Skating competitions
rely have set training
eriods when skaters are
pposed to practise. People
de whenever they feel like
and don't let anybody tell
em what to do.

Unfortunately the
creased commercialisation
f skateboarding threatens
change the very nature of
e sport. There is an ever-
creasing danger of it being
ought of as a show rather
an as a sport. This could
entually lead to
ateboarders founding their
wn association to fight for
eir interests. But whether
at will happen remains to
e seen.

Don Brown, *impossible to pogo*
(freestyle competition)

cky Guerrero from Denmark doing a *grind*
the halfpipe

FREESTYLE

Freestyle is the more artistic, dance-like form of of the sport. The skater performs his tricks to music on a flat surface, using a much narrower board. Just as in ice skating, he performs a two-minute routine that he's made up himself.

A good freestyle routine consists of a carefully coordinated sequence of difficult tricks combined with various stylistic movements (finesses) such as wheelies. The sequence should also fit in well with the music. A jury takes all these things into account when awarding points.

In recent years there's been one freestyle skater who has consistently led the field: Rodney Mullen from Florida. Significantly, he is one of the few skaters to have followed a well-organised training programme. Every minute on the board was carefully recorded in his diary, together with every new trick he invented. He was also one of the first skaters to undertake a full build-up programme of jogging, stretching exercises etc.

Rodney Mullen is the creator of modern freestyle. He combined outstanding talent with an iron discipline in training, with the result that he is still considered unbeatable today.

Different styles

Freestyle skating can take many different forms. Acrobatics such as the various handstands are very popular with the crowds, but these are often thought of as gymnastics rather than skating.

Then there is a whole series of so-called stationary tricks that don't involve any skating as such. The skater can stand in the normal position, or move to the edge of the board (railflips) the trucks (pogos) or the tail (Caspers) in a wide variety of ways.

By contrast, the so-called rolling tricks usually take place at speed, using the momentum of the board to produce wheelies or various complicated flips.

If you want to concentrate on stationary tricks, then you should tighten up the truck mountings on your board until they are rock-hard. This means you won't be able to steer the board by shifting your weight, but you'll find you can control the timing of your tricks much more easily.

If you prefer rolling tricks, you should always leave sufficient play in the trucks for steering, as this is particularly important for performing wheelies properly.

KICKFLIP

The kickflip is one of the oldest tricks in freestyle. The aim is to flip the board over using only your feet so that you can ride away afterwards.

↦ The starting position is different from the usual riding position. Hold your front foot over the side edge of the board so that it is effectively gripping it, and place your back foot so that the middle of it is over the opposite edge.

↦ Pull up sharply with your front foot to flip the board over, while at the same time pushing down with your back foot.

↦ While you're in mid-air, turn your body 90 degrees towards your back foot so that you land on the board in the normal riding position.

ROLLING FINGERFLIP

The rolling fingerflip is a fairly easy trick, and you can do it while you're moving quite slowly.

⌐ Start with your back foot in the normal riding position, and with your front foot half-way along the board with the toes placed in the middle.
⌐ Lean forwards and grab the nose with your front hand.

⌐ Jump up with your front foot first, pushing down on the tail with your back foot (there's no problem if the tail touches the ground).
⌐ When both feet are in the air, flip the board with your hand so that it rolls right over.
⌐ Land on the board in the normal riding position.

G-TURN

This is one of the nicest tricks in freestyle.

➤ Ride at medium speed and place your front foot on the nose of the board.

➤ Lean well forward over the front foot, bending your knees at the same time.

➤ As the back wheels lift off the ground, do a frontside turn, lifting your arms in the air to help you balance and using your back foot to control the position of the board.

➤ The board will turn more sharply as it slows down: turn it right round through 180 degrees and set off back in the opposite direction.

ROLLING 180 NO-HAND CASPER

This trick is easier to do if you stand back-to-front on the board, i.e. with your front foot on the tail and your back foot on the nose.

— Move slowly backwards, with your front foot on the edge of the board next to the truck and with your back foot (mainly the heel) on the nose.

— Push down with your front foot to turn the board upside-down.

— Land with your back foot on the underside of the nose, and hold the front of the board up with your front foot.

— Jump off the board while at the same time flipping the board over onto its wheels with your front foot.

— Land on the board in the normal riding position, turning your body slightly so as to land safely.

BUTTERFLIP

➝ You first have to get the board onto its side. You do this by using the instep of your back foot to pull up the edge of the board, while at the same time jumping up with your front foot.

➝ Now stand with your feet on the edge and wheels at the same time so as to make the board stable.

➝ Move your back foot over the tail and your front foot onto the back wheels to get ready for the flip.

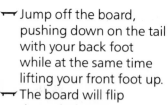

- Jump off the board, pushing down on the tail with your back foot while at the same time lifting your front foot up.
- The board will flip through three-quarters of a turn in the air. Grab the nose when the board is at the point where your back foot will land on the back truck.
- When your back foot lands there, kick forwards with your front foot.
- Use your front hand to flip the board through yet another 180 degrees so that you can land in the normal riding position.

SHOVE IT

- Ride in a straight line at a medium speed.
- Lean forwards over the nose so that the tail rises in the air.
- Shove hard against the tail to send the board swivelling around the front wheels through a complete 360-degree turn. Be careful to judge how hard you need to shove, and jump in the air to let the board turn freely.
- Land back in the normal position when the nose is pointing forwards again.

ROLLING IMPOSSIBLE

- Roll gently backwards with your feet positioned at the nose and tail.
- Lift your front foot and grab the nose with your instep, and the board will tip back onto its tail.
- Now swivel the board through 180 degrees so that you are facing forwards.

- Use the momentum from this to help flip the board over with your front foot. Provided you flip hard enough, the board will turn through a full 360 degrees, i.e. back onto its wheels.

- Land in the normal riding position as soon as it's safe to do so.

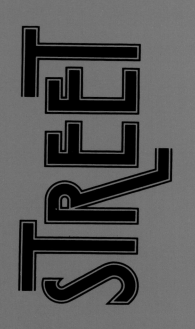

STREET

There are two kinds of skating involved here. One is street skating, which is ordinary skating around the streets of the town. The other is so-called street style – a competition discipline that tries to emulate street skating. In this book we will concentrate on street skating proper, because street style in competition has never really managed to match up to real-life skating on the streets.

Street is by far the oldest form of skateboarding, and its rediscovery in the mid-eighties is strongly associated with the name of Mark Gonzales of California. He was the first skater to adapt the vert ollie for use on the street, laying the foundation for a whole new development in the sport. The street ollie is a way of making the board take off by pushing down on the tail while pushing your front foot forward. This provides the ideal way of jumping onto or over various objects.

But street skating is much more than just hurdling with high ollies. The main aim is to use the whole of the street environment. Skaters aren't satisfied any longer with just cruising up and down the tarmac as they used to in the sixties and seventies. They want to skate over everything that they find in the street.

Kerbs are ideal for grinds and slide 'n' rolls. Steps and stairways offer a whole range of ollie variations, while the rails and walls can be used for practising handrail slides. Even the walls of buildings come into their own for wallriding, which means jumping onto the side of a wall and riding along it for short distances. You can also put a ramp against the wall to make it easier to mount. Mark Gonzales was one of the first of these enterprising skaters who turned the street into a kind of improvised skatepark. Since then street skating has taken off again. Skaters scorch along the streets and walkways, and the most unlikely obstacle becomes a skate spot where you can linger for hours trying out new, ever more radical tricks.

A street skater uses every opportunity that a street provides. Don Wilkes from America does a *slide 'n' roll* on a children's slide

180-DEGREE SLIDE

The 180-degree slide is an alternative method of braking on the street.

- Approach at medium speed, and lean back slightly onto your back foot.
- Press on the tail so that the back wheels start to skid on the tarmac.
- Lean back as you do this, and the board will do a 180-degree frontside turn around the back wheels.

If you keep your wheels on the ground throughout the manoeuvre, the friction will bring the board to a standstill.

STREET OLLIE

This ollie forms the basis for nearly all the other street tricks.

→ Ride in a straight line at a moderate speed.
→ Move your front foot back to about 6 inches behind the front truck and bend your knees slightly.
→ Push down hard on the tail with your back foot so that the front of the board springs in the air.
→ At the same time push your front foot forward so that its outer edge 'pulls' the whole board up into the air.
→ Now bend your legs close up against your body so that they effectively cushion your landing.

OLLIE TO TAIL

This trick starts in exactly the same way as the ordinary street ollie. But at the point where the board takes off you make a 180-degree frontside turn. You should time the manoeuvre carefully so that the tail lands on an adjoining step or kerbstone during the landing phase.

One possible variant of this is to land on the kerb in the Smith grind position, i.e. with the back truck and the toeside rail grinding on the kerb.

LIE TO GRIND

- Find a suitable sloping kerb or low wall to practise this trick on.
- Approach the slope at an angle and move into an ollie.
- During the 'flight phase', turn your board round to land parallel with the edge of the slope.
- Land on the wall with both trucks at the same time, and ride on down.

OLLIE TO DISASTER

- ↖ Approach a low wall head-on.
- ↖ Perform a high ollie so that your front wheels go over the wall and the board lands in the so-called disaster position.
- ↖ Take advantage of the forward momentum to pull the board up with your back foot.
- ↖ At the same time turn your front foot forwards and inwards so that the board comes to a halt in a frontside grind on the back truck.
- ↖ Now press down on both the nose and the tail in order to jump down off the wall.

SLIDE 'N' ROLL

⌐ Find a suitably smooth
wall or slippery railing
that you can slide down.
⌐ Approach at normal
speed parallel to the wall
or railing.
⌐ Jump onto the wall by
means of an ollie

combined with a
90-degree frontside
turn; try not to lean
backwards as you land.
⌐ Staying as upright as you
can, slide down the wall
a short way, gauging the
distance according to
the initial speed.
⌐ Push down on the tail to
jump down off the wall,
taking advantage of any
remaining momentum.

OLLIE GRAB

- Find a suitable raised area with an edge to jump off.
- Approach the edge at a fairly slow speed, and start an ollie just before you reach the brink.
- Just before the highest point of the flight phase, grab the board immediately behind the heel of your front foot.
- Land with your knees still bent and your feet over the trucks, and use your knees to cushion the fall and so prevent the board from breaking.

180-DEGREE OLLIE

This trick can be performed either on the flat or from a suitable edge (as in the pictures).

➤ Approach fairly slowly and start an ollie just before the edge.

➤ As you take off, swivel your body through a 180-degree frontside turn, pushing with your back foot and leaning slightly backwards to assist the turn.

➤ Complete the turn just before you land facing in the opposite direction; take care to cushion the fall by bending your knees.

NO-COMPLY

Very little momentum is needed to initiate this trick.

- Start an ollie, but as you press down with your back foot, take your front foot right off the board.
- Use your back foot to swivel the board through a 180-degree frontside turn using the back wheels, keeping your front foot on the ground and turning your body in line with your back foot; your legs will become splayed.
- Finish the trick by pushing off with your front foot and putting it back on the board.

NO-COMPLY REVERT

This is an interesting variation on the no-comply, and the first part of the trick is exactly the same. The new part begins at the point where you are nearly doing the splits, with your front foot on the ground, your back foot on the tail and the front wheels in the air.

This time keep the front wheels in the air and turn the board back again to its original position. Don't let the front wheels touch the ground again until your front foot is back on the board.

360-DEGREE VARIAL

➝ Roll the board slowly backwards with your front foot near the middle of the board.
➝ Push the tail down with your back foot as you step off the board with your front foot.
➝ As the nose jumps into the air, grab the board with your front hand while stepping off it with your back foot.

➝ Now turn the board through a whole 360 degrees.
➝ As you do this, turn your body back through 180 degrees and jump back onto the board as it lands.

OLLIE KICKFLIP

You should approach this trick slowly, and begin it in much the same way as an ordinary street ollie. But this time only let the toe of your front foot remain in contact with the board. This will cause the board to flip over completely during the flight phase. The effect will be heightened if you push down hard with your front foot at the point where you push down on the tail. The landing is again similar to an ordinary ollie.

57

MINIRAMP

At first sight a miniramp looks like a small halfpipe that's been cut off just below the vert. But if this leads you to believe that the miniramp isn't worth a fraction of the halfpipe, then you'd better think again, because miniramp skating is the 'in' sport.

Whole miniramp parks have sprung up, and each has its own rich and varied landscape made up of various ramps in umpteen different sizes and shapes. They might, for instance, include two miniramps laid back-to-back, with the two transitions linked by a double coping (spine) so that the skater can move easily from one ramp to the other.

Some people think the miniramp is only for beginners who want to build up a bit of confidence before venturing out onto the larger and more terrifying halfpipe. But this is a myth too. The miniramp, being lower, is admittedly less daunting than the halfpipe. But miniramp also has its own laws and skills that mark it out as a discipline in its own right. The main emphasis is on liptricks (see page 69), and skaters take a special interest in everything that goes on just below the coping.

Thus the miniramp has given a boost to halfpipe skaters, who are now trying to incorporate various liptricks in their own repertoire, especially the 'to revert', 'to fakie' and ollie – liptrick combinations. Such combinations were previously thought impossible, but miniramp skaters have shown they can be done, so that vert skaters are now trying them out again.

Miniramp, therefore, is in no way the 'poor relation' of halfpipe. It is a discipline on an equal footing, and what is more, it has established itself as a rich source of new ideas and tricks for vert skaters.

Above: a miniramp layout with a spine and a side section at the 1990 Scandinavian Open, Copenhagen. Left: Jan Waage from Hamburg. Right: 'Gator' Mark Anthony in a *feeble to fakie*

OLLIE GRAB TO FAKIE

- ↝ Start with your front foot well back towards the middle of the board.
- ↝ Set off up the ramp in a half-crouch position.
- ↝ Start a typical ollie by pushing down on the tail and bringing your front foot forward.
- ↝ When you reach the highest point, grab the board just behind your front heel, and at the same time push your front foot forward so your knee is straight – the nose-bone position.
- ↝ Fall back onto the ramp, and let go of the board just as you reach the coping; don't let go too early, or you risk not landing safely.

50/50 TO FAKIE

- Set off up the ramp in a slightly backside direction.
- Press on the tail so that the board turns through 90 degrees backside and the back truck hits the coping.
- Pull yourself upright as you place the front truck on the coping.
- Grind both trucks along the coping.
- As you lose speed, push down on the tail towards the bottom of the ramp, and turn your body through 90 degrees into the 'fakie' position.
- The back truck will leave the coping first; now turn the board back round, allowing the wheels to skid down the ramp surface, and roll backwards (to fakie) down the ramp.

body well forward over the nose as long as the back wheels are still ove the platform.

NEW DEAL

- Set off up the ramp in a slightly backside direction, with your front foot on the nose and slightly turned in.
- Just before you reach the coping, push down on the nose to raise the tail, and grind the front truck a short way along the coping.
- As you do this, lean forwards and inwards to

turn the board through 180 degrees until the tail is nicely balanced above the platform.

- When you've finished the turn, slide the front truck down off the coping, but keep your

- Don't bring the back wheels down until they've come safely ove the coping and you can roll smoothly back dow the ramp.

NE-FOOT BACKSIDE ISASTER

- Set off up the ramp in a slightly backside direction, and start an ollie with a 180-degree backside turn.
- As soon as the tail has left the ramp, kick forwards with your front foot.

- Time the turn carefully so that you land with the rails on the coping. But before landing your front foot should be back on the board, so the kick has to be a very fast one.

- Now push down on the nose with your front foot to bring the back wheels safely over the coping.
- Bring the back wheels down and roll back down the ramp.

SMITH GRIND

The Smith grind is exactly the same on the miniramp as in the halfpipe.

- Set off up the ramp in a slightly frontside direction.
- Lift your front wheels over the coping, then grind over the coping with the back truck, and pull yourself upright and over onto the platform.
- Turn your board through 90 degrees until you're running parallel to the top of the coping.
- Now push down on the nose so that the frontside rail grinds on the coping.
- Grind along the coping until you come to a halt or reach the end of the ramp.
- Make another 90-degree turn, push down on the nose and roll back down the ramp.

HALFPIPE

Halfpipe skating, or ramp riding as it's often called, is the most radical of all the skateboard disciplines, attracting spectators in their thousands. And yet at the same time it attracts the smallest number of actual skaters. Why should this be?

Firstly, tricks on the halfpipe are generally more difficult and dangerous than those in the other disciplines. You have to be able to control the board at very high speeds, often as much as 10 feet off the ground – and most street skaters and freestylers simply haven't got what it takes to do that.

But the main reason is a simple practical one. You can't learn the halfpipe without a halfpipe to practise on, and there just aren't enough of these around. The cost alone is enough to put people off building one. A halfpipe can cost anything from £4,000 to £20,000 to build, depending on its size and what it's made of. Not many clubs can afford this, and there aren't many authorities that are willing to subsidise one either. On top of that there is the high cost of insurance, and it isn't easy to get planning permission for such a 'high-risk' venture.

Building materials

Assuming you can find your way around all these problems, there's the question of building materials. A wooden structure is cheaper than a steel one, but much less weatherproof. If your halfpipe is going to be out in the open air, then the load bearing structures at least should be made of steel.

No less important is the choice of material for the running surface. A flexible kind of wood is the usual choice (e.g. 9-millimetre sheets of beech or plywood but a steel surface is also possible. Your choice will depend on several factors, including the money availab Steel is expensive but lasts longer; wood on the other hand gives much more grip

The layout

The ramp should measure least 15 to 16 feet (4.5 to 5 metres) wide, although 23 to 40 feet (7 to 12 metres) really ideal. But far more important is the length of the **transition,** which should measure about 10 feet (3 metres) from the en of the flat section to the beginning of the vertical.

The **vertical** should measure a further 8 to 16 inches (20 to 40 centimetre above the end of the transition. The vert is neede to bring you smoothly out the halfpipe for airs and oth tricks. It also helps you to lan safely again afterwards.

Gerd Rieger pushes the *boneless one* to its furthest limit

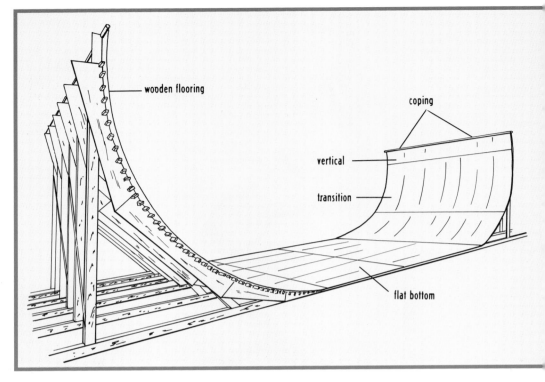

Labels on diagram: wooden flooring, coping, vertical, transition, flat bottom

The construction of a halfpipe

A good halfpipe is determined by the length of the transition in relation to the height of the vertical:

➤ If the transition is too short and/or the vert is too high, then the skating will become too fast.

➤ If the transition is too long, then too much effort will be needed to get up the necessary speed.

The **flat bottom** linking the two transitions should be about 13 to 16 feet (4 to 5 metres) long.

The coping

This is a metal pipe measuring about 3 inches (7 centimetres) in diameter that runs along the top of the vertical. It serves two important purposes:

➤ Liptricks such as grinds and lipslides are easier and therefore safer.

➤ It's vital at the beginning of any aerial trick (air). When your board leaves the halfpipe, the back wheels run up against the coping, pushing the board against your feet and giving you more control in mid-air.

The tricks

There are three main kinds of tricks in the halfpipe:

➤ airs (aerials);

➤ inverts;

➤ liptricks.

Airs are of course the mos spectacular of all the tricks With enough speed you ca jump off the halfpipe, turn through 180 degrees in mid-air, and land back safe on the halfpipe just below the coping. During the so-called flight phase, you gra the board with one hand t keep it steady. However, there are certain kinds of airs, known as ollie airs, in which you control the boar with just your feet.

Inverts can best be described as one-armed handstands. You grip the board with one hand, han onto the coping with the

r and swing upside-
n into the handstand
tion. Inverts, like airs,
ally involve a 180-degree
n in the air so that you
ne back down again
wards.

_iptricks are, as their
me suggests, tricks that
volve sliding over the
ping, either with the
ucks (grinds) or with the
ils underneath the deck
lides and disasters). There
re tailslides, too, in which
he tail runs over the coping.
'et another variant is the
footplant, in which you take
one foot off the board and
use it to push off from the
coping.

This three-way division is
only a very rough guide,
because new tricks are
appearing all the time, and
some of them won't fit into
any of the categories. In
recent years, for example,
skaters have started to
combine airs with liptricks.
You might start a trick, say,
with an ollie, but just before
landing you might pull the
board up over the coping
and slide along the edge for
a short distance. The result:
an ollie lipslide.

There are also subgroups
within each of the main
groups. The airs, for example,
include the so-called **varials,**
in which the board alone is
given an extra turn during
the flight phase.

Liptricks are now fast
overtaking the airs as the
most radical tricks. The
landing phase in particular
is varied to include 'to
revert' and 'to fakie'.

To revert is when you do an
extra 180-degree turn
during the final phase of the
trick so as to return down
the ramp backwards.

To fakie involves a turn at
the very beginning so that
you come down backwards.
Coming down backwards is
what makes these tricks so
difficult and radical.

The list of tricks could go
on for ever. Skaters on the
American pro scene seem to
invent new tricks practically
every day, so that even the

lfpipe skating is like the movement
a pendulum

experts can't really keep up with them. So for the purposes of this book we will limit ourselves to just the basic tricks that are used in the halfpipe.

Basic halfpipe skills

Before you do any actual tricks, there are some basic skills you need to learn first. The first of these is **vertical pumping,** which is the method used for getting up speed on the ramp. It can be approached in several stages.

The first time you use the halfpipe, start on the flat section by pushing off with your foot, and go a short way up the transition. The second time, let the board roll down and back up the opposite transition. Once you've got used to this pendulum motion, you can gradually start to build up speed.

Do this by making yourself as small as possible at the stall point (the top) of each swing, and standing upright as you approach the flat. Start bending your legs as soon as you meet the opposite transition, so that you are back in the crouching position by the time you stall again. The stall point will become progressively higher as your speed increases.

Practise this pumping technique until it's etched on your brain, and as automatic as using a knife and fork. This will also give you practice in riding **fakie,** or backwards, whether up or down the transitions.

Now you should be ready to start a few **kickturns** (see page 29). These shouldn't pose any problems, and you can include one each time you mount the transition. Always make sure to keep your body facing sideways on to the board. If you don' you'll always end up in a bai

The next important stage after vertical pumping, fakie and kickturns is the **drop-in,** which you start from the top of the ramp. Before starting, place your board across the edge of the platform with the back truck against the coping and the nose pointing down into the halfpipe.

First put your back foot or the tail, then place your fror foot in the basic riding position, and at first keep

Nicky Guerrero in a *lipslide*

ur weight on the back ot. Now lean well rwards onto your front ot, and push your front heels down onto the urface of the transition. This can be pretty scary at rst, but it's much safer to an too far forwards than t far enough, because if u bail you can land on ur kneepads (see page 27). ackwards bails are far more dangerous. The other advantage of leaning well forwards is that you'll naturally fall into the correct riding position, with your body facing sideways on to the board.

Once you've mastered all these basic skills, you'll be ready to start on some of the actual tricks. Now it's time for some real fun, so good luck and go for it!

Mark van der Eng doing a *frontside invert*

ris Miller goes over vert in the fullpipe at Upland

AXLE STALL

- Start by riding straight up the ramp.
- Just before the front wheels hit the coping, start a 90-degree backside kickturn, leading with your shoulders and raising the front wheels by slight pressure on the tail.
- The back truck should hit the coping as your body begins to turn, and during the turn the back truck will be your only point of contact with the halfpipe.
- As you finish the turn, pull your body upright above the platform and place the front truck on the coping.
- In order to get back down into the halfpipe, bend your knees slightly and kick the board through another 90-degree turn.

ROCK 'N' ROLL

➤ Start by riding straight up the ramp.

➤ Lift the front wheels over the coping by pressing slightly on the tail, and push the board over onto the platform.

➤ Straighten up a bit as you do this, and turn your body to face back down into the halfpipe as the back truck hits the coping.

➤ Push down on the tail to kick the board back round into the halfpipe, using the outside of your front foot to control the turn.

➤ As soon as the board's been turned round, drop back down and place your wheels back inside the halfpipe.

FAKIE OLLIE

This trick starts backwards and involves no turning.

⌐ Ride up the ramp backwards, tail first, and crouching slightly as you approach the top.

⌐ Just before the back truck reaches the coping, push on the tail slightly to raise the nose.

⌐ As the back wheels hit the coping, straighten your back foot so as to take full advantage of the coping as you're thrown into the air.

⌐ Pull your legs in at the highest point, and straighten them again as you're about to land.

⌐ Don't put your back wheels down again until they've passed the coping.

IN TO TAIL

➤ Ride up the ramp along a slightly frontside path.

➤ As the front truck reaches the edge, straighten your back leg and press hard on the tail; this will lift the front truck over the coping but push the back truck and tail hard against it.

➤ Grab the nose with your front hand as the board jumps off into the air.
➤ The angled approach will start the board turning; lead with your shoulders and hips to make it turn through a full 180 degrees.

➤ Throughout the turn, keep the nose of the board inclined down the ramp, and your feet firmly in contact with the board.
➤ Hit the tail against the coping as you land, and lean sharply forward to bring the board safely down onto the ramp.
➤ Ride back down the ramp.

LIPSLIDE

This trick is also known as a **frontside disaster.**

⌐ Mount the ramp at a slightly frontside angle.

⌐ As you approach the edge, turn slightly frontside into an ollie movement so that your back wheels hit the coping, knocking you into the air.

⌐ While you're in mid-air, turn your body through 180 degrees and use your feet to bring the board round.

⌐ When you reach the highest point, push the board towards the platform with both feet so that the rails land on the coping.

⌐ Now slide the rails over the coping.

⌐ To get back down, lean right forwards into the halfpipe and push down on the nose to lift the back wheels safely over the coping without getting them caught.

BACKSIDE DISASTER

The backside disaster is like the lipslide only the opposite way round.

↪ Mount the ramp in a slightly backside direction.

↪ As you approach the top, turn slightly backside into an ollie.

↪ When you've nearly finished the 180-degree turn, push the tail back over the platform to bring the rails down onto the coping; straighten your legs just before you land, and make sure your weight is over the platform.

↪ Drop back down again by leaning well forward onto the nose to lift the back wheels safely over the coping.

INVERT

- Start by riding straight up the ramp.
- Crouch down as you approach the coping, and grab the inside edge of the board with your front hand.
- When you reach the coping, hold onto it with your back hand to give you support.
- Pull the board right up over the coping, and

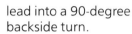

lead into a 90-degree backside turn.
- Carry your weight on the supporting arm, keep both feet firmly on the board, and swing the board up and over until it is parallel with the

coping (a one-armed handstand).
- To return to the halfpipe swing on down again, turning backside throug another 90 degrees.

ONTSIDE INVERT

- Ride up the ramp along a slightly frontside path.
- Crouch down as you approach the coping, and grab the outside edge of the board with your front hand.
- Lift the front wheels over the coping, and turn your body through 90 degrees, supporting yourself on the coping with your back hand.

⊢ Carry your weight on the supporting arm and swing yourself up into the one-armed handstand position, leaning more towards the platform than in the ordinary invert.

⊢ To come back down again, push yourself away from the coping with your supporting hand, turn through another 90° and bring the wheels back down onto the ramp.

LEIN AIR

↽ Mount the ramp along a sightly frontside route.

↽ Lift the front wheels over the coping, and grab the board with your front hand near the wheels and just ahead of your front foot.

↽ Knock the back wheels against the coping as you take off out of the halfpipe.

↽ While in mid-air, turn your body to bring you round through 180 degrees.

↽ As you reach the highest point of the flight phase, lean well back towards the bottom of the halfpipe.

↽ As you come down again, pull the nose down with your front hand until the board is almost vertical and the wheels can land safely on the ramp.

BACKSIDE AIR

➤ Ride up towards the coping in a fairly straight line.

➤ As you approach the coping, do the same as for all the other airs:
  - press on the tail to bring the front wheels over the coping;
  - grab the board with your front hand near the front wheels;
  - hit the back wheels against the coping as you take off.

➤ While in mid-air, swivel your body to lead into a 180-degree backside turn.

➤ As you reach the highest point in the air, straighten your back leg as far as possible to bring you into a horizontal position.

➤ As you come down to land, bend your back leg again and crouch forwards into the halfpipe.

FRONTSIDE BONELESS

⌐ Mount the ramp in a slightly frontside direction.

⌐ As you approach the coping, do three things at the same time:
  − crouch down and grab the middle of the board with your back hand;
  − lift the front wheels over the coping;

− take your front foot off the board and place it on the coping.

⌐ Now jump off the coping into mid-air, leading into a 180-degree frontside turn.

⌐ As you come down again, put your front foot back on the board, and let go with your hand as you pass level with the coping.

FASTPLANT

The fastplant is a combination of the backside air and the footplant.

- ➤ Ride straight up the ramp and lift the front wheels over the coping.
- ➤ Now do two things at the same time:
  - grasp the board as for the backside air (see page 81);
  - take your back foot off the board and push off hard from the coping.
- ➤ Lead into a 180-degree backside turn, just like an air except your back foot is off the board.
- ➤ Replace your back foot on the tail as you start to come down towards the ramp.

FEEBLE TO FAKIE

- Ride forwards straight up the ramp.
- As you reach the coping, push the board over onto the platform as for a rock 'n'roll to fakie (see page 73).
- But don't stop this movement until the back truck reaches the coping; then turn the board slightly backside and grind the back truck on the coping.

- Press on the tail to bring the board back down onto the ramp, and return backwards (fakie).

AIR TO FAKIE

↤ Ride in a straight line up the ramp.

↦ Do the same as in the backside air (see page 81): grasp the board near the front wheels and hit the back wheels against the coping as you take off.

↦ But this time, instead of turning, simply fall back towards the ramp.

↦ Make sure you let go with your hand as soon as you're certain you've passed the coping.

OLLIE STALEFISH

— Start this trick in the same way as an ordinary frontside ollie, jumping off the ramp into a 180-degree turn.

— As you start to turn, bring your back hand around behind your back leg and grasp the board somewhere about the middle (to do this you might have to angle your back leg towards the board so that the knee is almost in contact with the board).

— Once you've got hold of the board, straighten and arch your body back as much as you can.

— Make yourself smaller again as you come down, and let go of the board as you pass level with the coping.

Accidents and first aid

In every sport there are some injuries that are more common than others. In skateboarding, for instance, the main risk is to the ankles, knees, wrists and elbows.

Some of the worst damage is caused by bad first aid, which can slow down the healing process no end. So to help avoid such problems, here are some tips about the kinds of injuries to look out for and what to do about them.

Ankles

Ankle sprains and strains are among the commonest injuries. These usually involve no more than overstretching of the ligaments. But there may occasionally be one or even several torn ligaments, and you should always suspect this if there's a lot of swelling.

Ankle injuries are much commoner in street than halfpipe, mainly because the ground is so unpredictable. The various ollies, ramp and rail tricks all tend to cause accidents that affect the ankles.

So for street skating you should take extra care when choosing shoes, even if it means digging deeper into your pockets. It's vital to have plenty of padding and support around the ankles. And if you have a lot of trouble with ankle injuries, you should wear a support

bandage for every session (ask your doctor's advice about this).

Knees

The knee is a complicated joint full of ligaments, muscles and tendons, all of which give support whenever you move it. This means the knee is relatively unstable and vulnerable to injury, and the weakest parts are the ligaments and cartilages.

The main risks here are in the halfpipe, where you are always landing on your knees. If you're not careful, repeated injury can lead to serious cartilage damage and erosion of the joint surfaces. But this shouldn't happen if you always, but always, wear decent kneepads!

If the knee becomes swollen, then the injury may be serious. The doctor will need to extract some of the fluid that is causing the swelling. This will relieve the joint and remove some of the damaging substances. The doctor can also analyse the fluid to find out what the injury is.

Wrists

The wrists are less injury-prone in skateboarding than the ankles and knees. But there's one type of injury that you should always watch out

for, as it can lead to serious complications if it's not treated properly straight away: a broken wrist.

Wrist fractures are commonest in street skating, where they are caused by falling on your hands with your arms straight so that the wrist takes the full force of the impact. Sometimes more than one bone is broken, and nobody notices until it's much too late. By this time even wearing a pot isn't enough to mend it, and the only solution is an operation followed by an even longer period in plaster.

So whenever you fall on your hands and damage your wrist, get it checked out immediately by your doctor or local casualty department.

First aid

The immediate treatment for joint injuries can be summed up in the word 'RICE':

R Rest for the injured limb;
I Ice applied to the injury;
C Compression bandages;
E Elevation, or lifting up the limb.

First rest the injured limb completely, putting it up in a raised position (Rest and Elevation). Then bind the affected joint tightly in a crepe bandage soaked in water (Compression), and finally put a plastic bag full of e cubes directly over the ury site (Ice).

After about half an hour, osen the bandage and let e blood get to the injury for couple of minutes. Then ndage it up again as efore, and repeat the ocess every half-hour for ree hours. By this time a octor should have looked at e damage, worked out hat is wrong and told you hat further treatment is eeded.

fter-care
he RICE treatment is the ost vital factor in curing an jury and bringing full use ick to the joint. But the next ost important thing is after-re. People so often ignore e need for physiotherapy

(exercises, massages, electrotherapy), and yet this is vital to the healing process. If it's done properly, you may be skating again sooner than you expect. If not, you may be out of the running for much longer.

Preventing injury
Injuries cause a lot of problems and complications, and yet they can often be easily avoided. The answer is never to go skating without the right protection, whether out on the street or on a ramp.

We're talking here about all the gear described earlier on (see pages 24 – 26). But there are other things that may be useful, especially if you've been injured before.

An injured joint is often weak long after it's healed, so the best way to avoid a 'repeat performance' is to wear one of the special bands, braces or support bandages that are available.

Don't be fooled into thinking that wearing protection is 'uncool', even if there's a trend for doing radical tricks without it. There are better ways of boosting your image than playing Russian roulette with your body. If you're protected, you can really push the limits. If you're not, your skating career will most likely be spectacularly short.

Florian Böhm does a *roll-in* at the new pool in Münster, Germany

ce Mountain from Los Angeles a *tuck-knee invert*

Skateboard terms

There are lots of words in skateboarding that aren't found in any dictionary, or that are used in unusual ways. If you're new to the sport, you might find these confusing. So we've compiled a list of the most important ones so that you can find your way about without having to ask too many questions or show up your ignorance.

Some of the terms refer to items of equipment, such as the board and its components or the different layouts that you'll come across. But most are used for describing tricks. The various terms can then be combined to show the various elements that go to make them up, such as 'ollie lipslide to Smith grind to revert'.

If we'd wanted to give every existing trick, we could have filled this whole book with them. But this is a 'how-to' book, not a skateboarding dictionary! So we've limited ourselves to the main words that go together to describe the various tricks. A lot of tricks have been called after various people, so their names won't mean much on their own.

A: the relevant unit on a durometer, which shows how hard a wheel is
aerial or **air:** a trick in halfpipe, miniramp or bank skating in which the skater manoeuvres in mid-air

backside: the direction of the skater in relation to the ramp, i.e. when his heels are turned towards the coping (see also frontside)
backyard: originally one of the back gardens of California where the first pools and ramps were used for skating
bail: a fall (in the halfpipe, try to land on your kneepads)
baseplate: used for fixing the truck to the deck of a board
bionic or **bio:** a particularly radical trick
board royalties: the commission received by a pro skater for having his name given to a particular model of board

carving: a way of getting up speed in a pool by swinging up and down along a curved path
Casper: a freestyle trick that at one point involves holding the board upside-down between the tail and the middle
concave: the curved profi[l] of a skateboard deck that gives the rider more stabili[ty]
coper: a device for protecting the truck (not often used these days)
coping: the top edge of a halfpipe or miniramp, usually a metal pipe
curb: see kerb

deck: the wooden part of the board on which the skater stands
disaster: a liptrick in the halfpipe in which the rails underneath the deck slide over the coping

rop-in: when the rider ops off the edge into a alfpipe or miniramp

kie: when the skater rides ackwards on the board, or trick in the halfpipe where e skater rides backwards some stage to avoid a rn at the top

p: a freestyle trick in hich the board is flipped er using the feet

ee fall: when the rider lls from a height with the ard

eestyle: as in ice-skating, e more artistic form of the ort

ontside: the direction of e skater in relation to the mp, i.e. when his chest is rned towards the coping e also backside)

llpipe: a cylinder-shaped ructure in which the skater n ride beyond the vertical

G

oofy-footed: a skater's eferred position on the ard, i.e. when the right ot is placed in front wards the nose (see also gular-footed)

grind: a trick in which the truck grinds over the coping of a halfpipe or a street kerb (kerb grind)

grip tape: sticky tape with a rough outer surface that is stuck on top of the deck to stop your feet slipping

halfpipe: a skateboard layout shaped like a half-cylinder for performing radical tricks, often in mid-air

handrail: usually a stair-rail – a common site for performing slides on the street

hanger: the cross-piece of a truck to which the wheels are attached

hardcore: a term used in the early eighties to describe the most daredevil skaters – not so fashionable these days

hardrock maple: the kind of wood used for making the best decks

hardware: the board and all its associated components

invert: a trick in the halfpipe involving a one-armed handstand

jump ramp: a ramp used by skaters in street style for shooting into the air

kerb: a street kerb (or equivalent block or step) for performing tricks on

kerb grind: see grind

kicktail: the curved tail of a skateboard deck behind the back truck (important for steering and manoeuvring the board)

kickturn: a way of turning the board by pressing on the tail

kids: the term normally used for newcomers to the sport

kingpin: the part of the truck that links the hanger to the baseplate (the rubbers are mounted on it too)

knee gasket: worn under kneepads to stop them slipping off

lamination: when layers of wood (usually seven) are glued and pressed together to make the deck
liptricks: tricks in the halfpipe or miniramp that are performed around the coping

miniramp: the youngest skateboard discipline -- a small halfpipe without the verticals
move: another word for trick

nose: the front part of the deck
nosebone or **nose-saver:** a plastic cap for protecting the nose (no longer used much)
nose-bone position: a riding position in which the front foot is pushed towards the nose and the knee is straight

obstacle: a feature of street style (usually a ramp)
ollie: a kind of trick in which the board takes off by means of pressure on the tail and without the hands being involved

pipe: sometimes used to mean halfpipe
pogo: a trick in which the skater stands on one of the trucks
polyurethane: a material used for making skateboard wheels, also known as 'thane'
pool: a round hole in the ground covered in concrete that can be used for skating (based on the round-sided swimming pools of California that were emptied for use by skateboarders)
pro model: a model of skateboard deck that is sold under the name of a pro skater

radical or **rad:** when a tric is particularly successful or spectacular
rails: the protective rails along the bottom of a skateboard deck
ramp riding: a term often used for halfpipe skating
recap: a replaceable plasti cap for use on a kneepad
regular-footed: a skater's preferred position on the board, i.e. when the left fo is placed in front towards the nose (see also goofy-footed)
revert: when a halfpipe trick includes an extra 180-degree turn just befor the rider lands so that he comes down backwards
rolling trick: a freestyle trick that takes place while the board is moving (see also stationary trick)

S

...ape: a unique design of ...ck cut for a pro from a ...andard pressing (see pro ...odel)

...dewalk surfer: an old-...shioned term for a skate-...ard (from the time when ...was built out of a surfboard ...th rollerskates attached)

...ate medic: a doctor or ...ramedic at skateboard ...mpetitions

...ate shoes: shoes specially ...ade for skateboarders

...ate zines: small photo-...pied mags produced by ...aters themselves

...de: a trick in which the ...ls of a board slide on the ...ping, or where the wheels ...id sideways instead of ...rning

...ace pad: extra padding ...tween the truck and deck ...give more clearance

...ine: double coping, used ...link two ramps laid back-...back

...ationary trick: a freestyle ...ck in which the board ...mains stationary (see also ...ling trick)

...reet: short form for street ...ating or street style (see ...low)

...reet skating: ...ateboarding out on the ...eets

...reet style: a competition ...scipline that imitates street ...ating

 T

tail: see kicktail

tailbone or **tailsaver:** a plastic cap for protecting the tail (no longer used much)

transition: the rounded part of a halfpipe, miniramp or bank (the term also applies to the radius of the transition)

truck: a skateboard axle

 V

vert or **vertical:** the short vertical section of the halfpipe above the transition

vert skating: a term that includes both halfpipe and pool skating

 W

wallriding: skating along a wall

wheelie: a freestyle trick in which you ride on two wheels only

Index

Where there are several page numbers, the main reference is shown in **bold type**. The index doesn't include references to the list of skateboarding terms.

Take up Sport

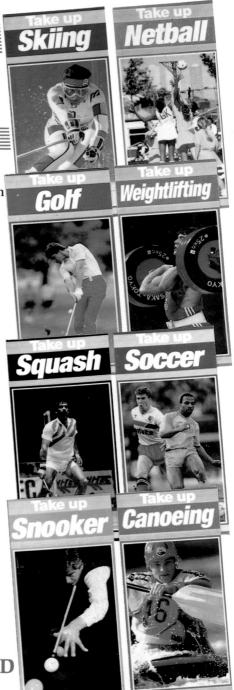

The Take up Sport series is the perfect introduction to sport, as well as explaining the basic rules each book provides hints and tips on techniques and strategy so that the newcomer can enjoy the game right from the start. Each book is written by an acknowledged expert in the sport. 210 × 100mm 48-64 pages black and white photographs and many line drawings second colour inside £2.95 Paperback

The books can be obtained from most good booksellers or directly from

SPRINGFIELD BOOKS LTD
Norman Road, Denby Dale, Huddersfield
HD8 8TH West Yorkshire. Tel: (0484) 864955
Fax: (0484) 865443